BEARS OF THE WORLD™

BLACK BEARS

DIANA STAR HELMER

The Rosen Publishing Group's
PowerKids Press™
New York

Many thanks to Don Middleton, member of the International Bear Research and Management Association, International Wildlife Rehabilitation Council, and founder and webmaster of The Bear Den, at http://www.nature-net.com/bears/

Published in 1997 by The Rosen Publishing Group, Inc.
29 East 21st Street, New York, NY 10010

First Edition

Book Design: Danielle Primiceri

Photo Credits: Cover shots © Mark Newman/International Stock, © Ronn Maratea/International Stock; p. 4 © Joanna McCarthy/Image Bank; p. 7 © Ron Maratea/International Stock; p. 8 © Joe Van Os/Image Bank; p. 11 © Scott Wm. Hanrahan/International Stock; p. 12 © AP/Wide World Photos; p. 15 © Bill Hickey/Image Bank; p. 16 © Ocean Images, Inc./Image Bank; p. 19 © Mark Newman/International Stock; p. 20 © Harald Sund/Image Bank.

Helmer, Diana Star, 1962–
    Black bears / Diana Star Helmer.
        p.   cm. — (Bears of the world)
    Includes index.
    Summary: Describes the physical characteristics, habitats, and interactions with humans of black bears.
    ISBN 0-8239-5132-4
    1. Black bear—Juvenile literature. [1. Black bear. 2. Bears.] I. Title. II. Series: Helmer, Diana Star, 1962– Bears of the world.
    QL737.C27H444 1997
    599,78'5—dc21   96-53249
                                                                                                                    CIP
                                                                                                                    AC

Manufactured in the United States of America

Table of Contents

What Color Are Black Bears?

Black bears live all over the world. **Asiatic** (ay-shjee-AH-tik) black bears live in China, Japan, Russia, Korea, and India. They have shaggy, black fur. A light-colored moon shape often grows in the fur on their chests. They have large, round heads, and big ears.

American black bears live in the United States, Canada, and Mexico. They have flat heads. Their noses point down. Their fur may be black, brown, blond, red, or gray. Black bears can even be white!

We know a lot about American black bears. **Scientists** (SY-en-tists) are still studying and learning about Asiatic black bears. The rest of this book will be about American black bears.

◀ *Black bears come in all different colors, including brown.*

Bears with Black Fur

When Europeans first came to North America, they saw bears that looked different from European bears. The American bears had black fur. They were smaller, weighing between 100 and 800 pounds. They had flat backs. And they loved to climb trees. American black bears were named for the color of the first bears that the Europeans saw. Later, people found other bears in North America that looked and climbed like black bears. These bears were all different colors, but they were still called black bears. Years later, scientists learned that black bears are alike on the inside no matter how different they look on the outside.

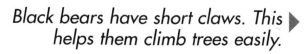

Black bears have short claws. This helps them climb trees easily.

A Bear's Territory

American black bears live almost anyplace that has small forests and streams. Many American black bears make their home in United States **national** (NASH-uh-nuhl) parks.

In the wild, each bear has its own **territory** (TEHR-ih-TOHR-ee). Black bears scratch on trees to mark their special places. Bears share the areas where they find their food, but they don't like to eat together.

◀ *Bears usually like to live alone in their own territories.*

Hungry as a Bear

Bears are **omnivores** (AHM-nih-vohrz). They eat almost anything! But most of the meals they eat are made up of plants. Bears eat berries, mushrooms, grass, flowers, roots, and nuts. They also eat bugs, eggs, birds, and fish. Bears even eat dead animals they find. This helps keep the forests clean.

In the fall, bears eat almost all day and night. Their fur grows thick and warm. A bear might gain as much as 30 pounds in one week during the fall. Bears must be fat to **hibernate** (HY-ber-nayt), or sleep, all winter.

*Some black bears like to hunt in ▶
nearby water for fish to eat.*

The Big Sleep

Bears hibernate because it is hard to find food in the winter.

A hibernating bear needs a den to sleep in. Bears can make dens out of caves or trees. Some bears let falling snow pile up around their bodies. Then the bear is snuggled up inside a den made of snow.

Hibernating bears breathe slowly. Their hearts beat slowly, too. The colder the winter is, the longer the bears sleep. They come out of their dens in April or May. Bears that weighed 300 pounds in the fall might weigh only 200 in the spring. They don't eat much at first. Their stomachs feel small. But soon the bears are hungry omnivores again.

◀ Bears that live in areas that stay warm during the winter don't have to hibernate. They can find food all through the winter.

Baby Bears

Grown bears **mate** (MAYT) during the summer. After a male and female mate, babies can start growing in the female's body. The babies don't grow much until the female is ready to hibernate. Then they grow quickly.

In January or February, sleepy mother bears have cubs. They help the blind babies find their mother's milk. Most bear mothers have two cubs. But some mothers have three or four cubs.

The new cubs drink milk and sleep in the winter den. They grow. After only two months, cubs can see, walk, and play.

Bears cubs are the last to come out of the den in the ▶ spring. They like to play in the warm spring weather.

Growing Up

New cubs are the last bears to come out in the spring. They are as little as teddy bears. A mother bear keeps her cubs safe from harm. She teaches her cubs to climb trees to reach safety, and to find food. By fall, cubs don't drink milk anymore. They eat a lot. They are getting ready to hibernate with their mother.

Cubs leave their mother when she mates again the next summer. The young bears may live together for one more winter. Then each bear finds its own territory.

◀ *Cubs learn to climb trees when they are young.*

Are People Safe from Bears?

Every bear is different. Bears are like people that way. Some bears are quiet. Others are grumpy. But every bear is wild. Wild animals are best left alone.

If you go into the woods, make noise as you walk to let any black bears in the area know you are coming. Bears usually stay away from people. But a surprised bear, especially a mother bear, might **attack** (ah-TAK).

Sometimes bears don't run because they smell food. If you're in or near a forest, always put food and garbage in an **airtight** (AYR-tyt) container. Never keep food in the area where you are sleeping.

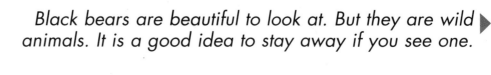

Black bears are beautiful to look at. But they are wild animals. It is a good idea to stay away if you see one.

Are Bears Safe from People?

Hundreds of years ago, people in China learned that part of a bear's body could help sick people. The bear's **gall bladder** (GALL BLA-der) could be made into a medicine. Many bears were killed for their gall bladders.

Today, medicine can be made without killing bears. Many countries have laws against using or selling medicine made from bears. But some people still want the bear's gall bladder. Others like soup made from bears. And some people just like to hunt them. Hunters who want money for the bears' gall bladders or bear soup kill more bears than is **legal** (LEE-gul).

◀ *There are more black bears in North America than any other kind of bear.*

Life with Bears

People can cause trouble for bears. In many countries, such as the United States, it is legal to hunt black bears. People also cut down trees in forests. They put up buildings where bears live. People camp in the woods where bears live. The bears move deeper into the woods, but the woods are getting smaller every day.

Some people want to help keep bears safe. They put their money together to buy wild land for bears. Other people use less paper and **recycle** (ree-SY-kul) paper. This helps save trees in the forests where bears live. People and bears must learn to live together without hurting each other's homes or lives.

Glossary

airtight (AYR-tyt) Something that keeps the air out and the smells in.

Asiatic (ay-shjee-AH-tik) From the continent of Asia, one of the largest masses of land on Earth.

attack (ah-TAK) To hurt or bite.

gall bladder (GALL BLA-der) A part of an animal's body that helps the animal get energy from food.

hibernate (HY-ber-nayt) To sleep all winter without eating.

legal (LEE-gul) Allowed by law.

mate (MAYT) A special joining of a male and female body. After mating, the female may have a baby grow inside her body.

national (NASH-uh-nuhl) Belonging to all the people of a country.

omnivore (AHM-nih-vohr) Something that eats both plants and animals.

recycle (ree-SY-kul) To use again.

scientist (SY-en-tist) A person who is an expert in some area of science.

territory (TEHR-ih-TOHR-ee) A space that an animal or group of animals takes as its own.

Index